FIVE-MINUTE MINDFULNESS

Parenting

FIVE-MINUTE
MINDFULNESS

Parenting

essays and exercises for
parenting from the heart

Claire Gillman

FAIR WINDS

Inspiring | Educating | Creating | Entertaining

Brimming with creative inspiration, how-to projects, and useful information to enrich your everyday life, Quarto Knows is a favorite destination for those pursuing their interests and passions. Visit our site and dig deeper with our books into your area of interest: Quarto Creates, Quarto Cooks, Quarto Homes, Quarto Lives, Quarto Drives, Quarto Explores, Quarto Gifts, or Quarto Kids.

Conceived, designed, and produced by
Quid Publishing
Part of The Quarto Group
Level 1 Ovest House
58 West Street
Brighton BN1 2RA
England

Design and layout by Lindsey Johns
Illustrations by Tilly and Tonwen Jones

Printed in Singapore

For our sons,
Alex and George, who gave
me and Nick the joy of
parenthood, and for parents
everywhere whose mindfulness
and love is cherishing and
guiding the next
generation.

Contents

Introduction

WHAT IS MINDFULNESS?

Mindfulness is a way of being. It is about being aware (or mindful) of what is happening around you and bringing your attention to that moment and that experience, without bestowing any sort of judgment on it. In mindfulness, you use all the senses to become aware—so you listen, you sense, you notice details, and you feel. And in doing so, you become present, living moment by moment. In mindfulness, you also become aware of, and take note of, your emotions and then you let them pass without acting on them. It's not that you ignore distracting thoughts and feelings exactly—rather that you acknowledge them without judgment or worry.

In mindfulness, techniques and exercises can be used to help you to better understand yourself and others. Meditation and contemplative thought are just some of the ways in which you can make sense of the thoughts and emotions you observe when you are present.

Mindfulness has its roots in Buddhism and it is just one of the many practices that make up the Buddhist philosophy. It wasn't until the early 1990s that the mindfulness element of Zen and Buddhist teachings was made available to the masses as a way of managing stress. Now there are several mindfulness-based therapies, such as Mindfulness-Based Cognitive Therapy, that are used to benefit psychological disorders and illnesses such as anxiety, trauma, addiction, and obsessive compulsive disorder (OCD).

The principles and practice of mindfulness can be applied to good effect in every aspect of life from breathing to walking to eating. Yet, it is when mindfulness is used by parents in relation to their children that it really comes into its own, because mindful parenting benefits not only your children—enormously I might add—but also yourself. Through mindful parenting, you can help your child to grow and develop in a safe, nurturing environment and, in the process, you will learn so much about yourself.

Why Parenting Can Be Stressful

Arguably, there has never been a more challenging time to be a parent. Most of us are fully paid-up members of the rat race, leading pressurized and stressful lives. Add children into the equation and the stress levels soar. Not only have you got to fit too much into your own work and social schedule, but now as parents, you have to fit your children and their needs into your life. Even before they start school there is pressure for your kids to attend the right activities, and the fear of them missing out or falling behind is a strong imperative even at this early age.

In the American Psychological Association's 2015 survey, *Stress in America: Paying With Our Health*, 47 percent of parents cited family responsibilities as a source of stress which manifests as irritability or anger, anxiety, and feeling overwhelmed.

There is so much to juggle in modern life, and having a child takes the pressure on your time to a whole new level.

The report quotes financial pressure as one of the major causes of stress for parents. Yet, for many, the greatest concern of all is the intrusion of the media and social media in their family lives. A National Opinion Polls study in Britain found that four out of five children under six years old watch up to six hours of television a day. Of 750 parents surveyed, two-thirds admitted that they use the TV as an "electronic babysitter." As children grow up, they become more engrossed in social media, feeling socially excluded if they do not participate. Teens and tweens in the U.S. are getting around nine hours' screen time a day, with some 13-year-olds checking social media 100 times a day, according to a report by Common Sense Media.

All of these factors conspire to make modern-day parenting a fraught challenge. For many, the cycle of unproductive behavior you witness in your children is not how you ever envisioned parenthood would be.

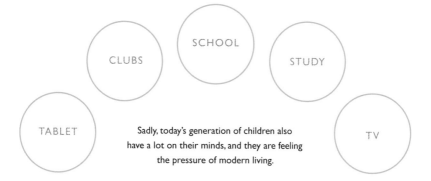

Sadly, today's generation of children also have a lot on their minds, and they are feeling the pressure of modern living.

Benefits of Mindfulness

Mindfulness is now promoted through meditation courses at universities such as Harvard and Brown, and recommended by the UK's Department of Health, as it is known to:

- Reduce feelings of stress and anxiety

- Increase feelings of calm and relaxation

- Aid chronic pain relief

- Improve self-confidence and self-esteem

- Increase energy levels and a sense of well-being

- Boost compassion for self, others, and our planet

HOW MINDFUL PARENTING CAN HELP

Mindful parenting is about parenting in an openhearted way—guiding and nurturing your child rather than dictating behavior. Of course, we all harbor ideas of how our children will turn out, but if you feel the need for yours to behave or be a certain way, and you are unwavering in this view, it can only lead to sorrow for you both.

Don't think the mindful parent never gets ruffled or is always calm. As a mindful parent, you are more aware of what is happening though. You learn to respond, not react. You notice when your buttons are being pushed and by being present find a better way to respond.

You are giving your child a secure emotional foundation. Using compassion, empathy, acceptance, and emotional intuition, in the good times and bad moments, your children are nurtured and grow healthily. And your self-understanding grows too.

At times, parenting will still be challenging, and even painful, but these moments help us to see our kids more clearly and to understand them better. If you dwell too much in the past or fret about the future, you are mentally absent and your child will feel it. To be a mindful parent, you don't have to be with your children constantly, but when you are with them, you make sure they have your attention. Paying attention—mindfulness—takes a lot of concentration. It is tiring, but the rewards make it well worthwhile.

About This Book

As a time-pressed parent who wants a better and more mindful way to raise your children, this book offers you brief essays on various aspects of mindful parenting that can be easily read and digested, plus simple exercises that, in keeping with the fast pace of modern life, only take five minutes to complete. Cherry-pick the bits that resonate well with you, and enjoy a new and rewarding way of interacting with your child.

"BY SEEING THE PAST
I GAIN NOTHING.

BY KNOWING THE FUTURE
I GAIN SOMETHING.

BY LIVING IN THE PRESENT
I GAIN EVERYTHING."

—SRI CHINMOY

① FINDING CALM

If the statistics are to be believed, there's a good chance you are feeling the stress of family life and the pressure to be a "good parent." Most of us prefer to think that we are in control at all times and don't like to admit that our stress levels are high. Yet, realistically, stress-free parenting is almost unheard of.

Whether you simply do not realize you're stressed, or you're trying to put a brave face on it, the truth is that acknowledging the situation is the first step in managing stress and your stress responses. Once you are aware that the pressure you feel is causing you to respond in unhelpful ways to your child's behavior, it becomes much easier to change your response. In turn, as you become calmer, shout less, and connect more, your children's frustrating behavior will become less frequent (or at least less irritating), and they will be more cooperative and connected.

Calming Down

There are several ways to reduce stress so you can start to be more mindful.

- Don't be afraid to ask for help and accept any offers of assistance that come your way. If family and friends are not close, prioritize paying for outside help rather than face the stress of taking it all on your own.

- Build in time for enjoyable activities for you and for all the family.

- Allow plenty of time—plans involving children take longer, and you'll be less stressed if you're not running late.

Professional Help

Most parents respond well to these stress-relieving tips, but for some, managing parenting stress on your own is simply too daunting, or events such as a family death or unexpected change can make it too much to deal with. In this case, it can be helpful to seek out a counselor, psychologist, or therapist to lend you support.

- Implement systems and don't rely solely on memory. Write lists, use diaries, get organized, so that you're not trying to find a gym bag as you leave the house in the morning. It is everyday chaos such as this that can cause the greatest levels of parental stress.

YOU REAP
WHAT YOU SOW:

YOUR CHILDREN MODEL THEIR BEHAVIOR ON YOUR BEHAVIOR. IF YOU USE YOUR PHONE OR SCREENS INCESSANTLY, THEN DO NOT BE SURPRISED WHEN THEIR TECHNOLOGY USAGE MIRRORS OR EXCEEDS YOUR OWN.

- Be kind to yourself—it's not the end of the world if the vacuuming doesn't get done or the grass doesn't get mown. These things are extras, not essentials.

- Learn to say "no"—turn down invitations, requests, and extra projects. It's not easy, but you need that extra time for yourself and your family.

- Make sure you get enough sleep and enough exercise. You think you don't have enough time, but you do!

Creating a Relaxing Home

Making sure your home environment is relaxing for you and your family is something that is often overlooked. Yet, making sure that your children have space for relaxation and occasional solitude is beneficial in helping them to feel safe and unpressured at home.

Obviously, not all homes are conducive to offering every member his or her own room, but even so, give thought to how your children can get away from the hubbub of family life if they feel the need for some quiet contemplative thought or me time.

One of the easiest places to restore calm is in your child's bedroom. Make sure it is not over-functional and over-stimulating. If it's equipped with a computer, TV, desk, and exercise equipment, then it is not going to be ideal for rest, relaxation, and sleep. Similarly, if a TV or radio is constantly on, then turn them off. Get your child used to peace and quiet. If you hate a silent house, then at least think about tuning in to a calmer background TV or radio channel.

Avoiding Media Madness

Technology is part of the modern childhood, but learning to manage its use can help to create a home that facilitates mindful living.

• Keep preschool kids away from TV and computer screens for as long as possible, and once they are at school, try to limit viewing and playing times, especially during the week. Can you find a creative alternative to occupy them— dressing up, coloring, making? Or something active—sports, games, outdoor play?

• Not all TV is bad—be selective with what your child watches and it can be educational or informative, as well as entertaining. You can also make it something that you do together. As your children get older, having a show that you always watch as a family offers an opportunity to interact and do something fun together.

• Get into the habit from the outset of only allowing phone chargers in a communal area. This might help to prevent the dangers of sleep deprivation from texting or talking too long at night when they move into their teen years.

Introducing Meditation

In a nutshell, mindful meditation is a way to focus on the present moment, using slow breathing techniques in a quiet space. It will benefit both you and your children if you can incorporate mindful meditation in your daily lives (failing that, some quiet time for contemplative thought is also beneficial). Just five minutes of mindful meditation a day can help to:

REDUCE STRESS LEVELS

MAKE YOU HAPPIER

IMPROVE YOUR APPRECIATION OF LIFE

MAKE YOU FEEL MORE CONNECTED

IMPROVE YOUR BRAIN FUNCTION

INCREASE YOUR ATTENTION SPAN

IMPROVE SLEEP QUALITY

INCREASE IMMUNITY

MINIMIZE AGING

TAKE FIVE GETTING STARTED

For adults, it's recommended that you sit in an upright chair, with your eyes shut and with your palms facing the sky. Take a moment to become aware of your surroundings and your body—how are you feeling? What can you hear?

Now draw your attention to your breath. Breathing through the nose, lengthen each breath, and observe it moving from your nostrils to your throat and then lungs, and back. Your mind may wander but gently draw it back to focusing solely on your breath.

Breathe 10 to 15 times, with full concentration on the breath. Then slowly bring yourself back into the room, and take a moment to see how your body and mind feels. Daily practice makes it easier each time.

For your children, it's best to introduce the idea as a game rather than give them a lesson in mindful meditation—a tricky concept for young children. Similarly, telling them to concentrate on their breath is generally not of interest, so this gentle exercise is a great way to start:

Ask your child to choose one of his favorite soft toys and then to lie down on his back. Get him to balance the toy on his tummy. Then ask him to watch the toy rising and falling as he breathes in and out—a simple but effective introduction to mindful meditation.

Noting Down Recurring Stress

Children are not always aware that they are experiencing stress. Getting them to note down the thoughts that consistently niggle in the back of their mind can be helpful. Once your child has made a note of what is troubling her, ask her to jot down how she reacts to it, or how it makes her feel. For example, "I often worry about whether my classmates like me, and so I think . . . and it makes me feel . . ." or "I sometimes worry about not being good at sports, and so I think . . . and it makes me feel . . ."

"WE CAN EASILY
MANAGE IF WE WILL ONLY
TAKE, EACH DAY, THE BURDEN
APPOINTED TO IT. BUT THE LOAD WILL
BE TOO HEAVY FOR US IF WE CARRY
YESTERDAY'S BURDEN OVER AGAIN
TODAY, AND THEN ADD THE BURDEN
OF THE MORROW BEFORE WE ARE
REQUIRED TO BEAR IT."

—JOHN NEWTON

These lists can help to give you and your children an insight into the thoughts that regularly churn in their minds and their usual reactions to them. Now explain to your child that you can choose to engage with these thoughts, or simply notice them and let them go. Stress that it is up to her whether or not she believes them or just recognizes them as unwanted thoughts that will pass on by.

Visualization Trick

If certain thoughts continue to worry and upset your children, practice this with them. Say to them:

See the thought that is worrying you and, as you breathe out, see it leaving the head and floating off with the breath. Each time you calmly breathe out, you can let go of any troubling thoughts.

Or:

You can visualize putting the troubling thought into a cookie jar. Then put the lid on the jar and put it back into the cupboard. In this way, you can know that the thought is now out of your head.

Finding the Still Point

Childhood at the end of the last millennium was relatively idyllic compared to the high-pressure, success-oriented, media-savvy world faced by today's children. A 2013 poll conducted by the Harvard School of Public Health found that almost 40 percent of parents said their high-school kid was experiencing a lot of stress from school. Even from a young age the pressure to excel academically makes children feel as if they are constantly doomed to failure.

Children also worry about bullying, sibling rivalry, parents getting divorced, moving house, and peer pressure. Although these are common parts of growing up, children do not have the emotional resources to cope with and process this stress. In addition, today's children have less free time to relax and so ordinary problems can become magnified and harder to deal with. As a mindful parent, you can give your children the vocabulary, the opportunity, and the tools to help them to identify, express, and process their thoughts.

Relentless high pressure on children can have far-reaching effects:

MAGNIFIED PROBLEMS

PERCEIVED STRUGGLE

REPRESSED FEELINGS

REPETITIVE WORRIES

STOP THE THOUGHT TRAIN

TAKE FIVE

Ever tried to stop your thoughts? Try this game with your children.

Give one person the stopwatch. The rest of the family closes their eyes and tries to empty their heads of thoughts. When 15 seconds is up, the timekeeper stops the game.

How did everyone get on? If you're honest, you will all find that it is almost impossible to stop your thoughts. Once your children realize that all of us have constant thoughts, you can then show them that you can think of thoughts as passing clouds. When negative thoughts are threatening to overwhelm your children, they can stop listening and let the thoughts pass—just as the clouds scud across the sky and pass. In doing so, your kids learn that the thoughts they tell themselves— "I think I'm ugly," "I think the other kids hate me," "I think I'm going to fail my exams"—are not always true, and they do not have to believe them. They can let them go like passing clouds.

2 MAKING TIME
(FOR THEM AND YOU!)

Have you ever seen the bumper sticker: Mom's (or Dad's) Taxi? For many parents, a large part of the experience seems to be driving to and from various activities and social events on their kids' over-stuffed schedules. In the main, these hectic timetables occur because parents worry that their child may fall behind if they don't attend the same enrichment activities as other kids.

However, the reality is that all this stimulating and structured activity— including watching TV or playing on devices—is affecting your children's mental state. They almost perpetually operate at a heightened state of alertness, and this is triggering stress responses. As your child rushes from one planned activity to the next, less and less time is available for just being and playing. Adults find it hard to be in the present moment, and by overscheduling our children's lives from an early age, we're quashing their natural instinct to live in the present moment too.

Children and Play

Children need to play. They need to get muddy and messy and to be allowed to explore through their play. Making mud pies, playing with water or sand, splashing in puddles—it all benefits their senses and their creative minds in a way that a screen or a programmed class never can.

Most importantly, children need to play unstructured games, because those activities that we deem as "leisure" can in fact be overstimulating when they are adult-led and involve following rules.

TIMETABLE REVIEW

TAKE FIVE

Take five minutes to draw up a schedule of your child's normal week, with the days of the week across the top, and hour or hour-and-a-half time slots down the side. Then fill in the timetable with all of his activities and commitments. If you use one color for stimulating activities and another color for calming activities, it will soon become apparent just how out of kilter the day is and how little downtime your child has during a normal week.

Typically, a child might only have an hour a day of unstructured playtime, half an hour for dinner, and an hour for bath time and a bedtime story. Two and a half hours per day is not a lot of downtime. The rest of his waking hours are filled with structured activities and stimulating screen time—so it should come as no surprise that children have tantrums and can't sleep: they are constantly "on the go" and feeling wired.

> *"IT IS PARADOXICAL THAT MANY EDUCATORS AND PARENTS STILL DIFFERENTIATE BETWEEN A TIME FOR LEARNING AND A TIME FOR PLAY WITHOUT SEEING THE VITAL CONNECTION BETWEEN THEM."*
>
> **—LEO F. BUSCAGLIA (DR. LOVE)**

Making Time (For Them and You!)

Building Family Time into a Hectic Schedule

It's not enough to wish you had more time to spend with the kids while they are little. Wishing alone will not change the situation. You have to actively free up some time in your life, expressly to spend time with the family.

The only way for this to happen is to slow things down, to take a few deep breaths, and to draw your awareness to how often you try to squeeze too much into your day. Become aware of the rhythm of family life and think about how a multiplicity of commitments is stopping you from being present and connected at important times. Don't over-pack the weekends and holidays. Be conscious when it is about to be a pressurized time for the kids and avoid scheduling other big events at that time. It takes mindful attention to balance and adjust your timetable successfully.

In all probability, the only way to get this kind of free time in your schedule is to let go of some of the things that you usually commit to. You cannot attend every class, meeting, or social event and still create space in your life for family time. You have to make choices and to learn to say no to requests and invitations. That's not to say you have to become a hermit—still say yes to the things that bring you joy—but by focusing your attention on what you actively want to make time for and declining the rest, you will be surprised at how much extra time you can find to engage and connect as a family.

Making Time (For Them and You!)

Hanging Out

When was the last time your kids had a kick about in the garden? No rules, just a bit of fun? Or built sandcastles on the beach? Or created a futuristic city out of blocks or Lego? Or just had time to sit and daydream?

Free play—where children are able to use their imaginations and think creatively to solve problems in different ways—has been shown to benefit kids when dealing with problems in later life, and also to improve academic performance in high school. Yet, the most important thing about free play is that it's fun.

One of the biggest criticisms of modern parenting is our need to micromanage and supervise every aspect of our children's lives. Why not give your children a chance to amuse themselves? Let them hang out with friends or on their own and let them find things to do rather than telling them what or how to do something, or finding ways to entertain them.

Building some unstructured time into your child's day will benefit her socially and cognitively. By allowing your child to explore, play, and make choices, and to work out solutions to her own problems, you are helping her to become resourceful and resilient.

Like most parents, we had to fight the urge to respond to cries of "There's nothing to do!" with suggestions, structure, and getting involved with entertaining the boys ourselves—instead we learned to leave them to their own devices. The younger son soon found that drawing and modeling the amazing creative ideas in his head was both absorbing and fulfilling. The older son would lose himself in a world of daydreams and write fantasy stories that were often sparked by the books he so loved to immerse himself in. Together, they would play intricate make-believe games too, often based on *Star Wars* or *Lord of the Rings*.

"WE ARE NEVER MORE FULLY ALIVE, MORE COMPLETELY OURSELVES, OR MORE DEEPLY ENGROSSED IN ANYTHING THAN WHEN WE ARE PLAYING."

—CHARLES E. SCHAEFER, CHILD PSYCHOLOGIST

Making Time (For Them and You!)

Recharging the Brain

What message are you sending to your child if you always refer to downtime—or any time that isn't answering emails or housework—as "time-wasting" or "being lazy"? How often does your child see you taking time to do a hobby that gives you pleasure—reading a book, doing some art, riding your mountain bike, sewing, tinkering in the shed, or gardening?

Remember to take time to notice morning dew on a cobweb or a spectacular sunset, and point it out to your child. Share the things you love with your child—so if gardening is a favorite pastime, why not get your child involved in planting up pots or growing vegetables? How about baking or cooking together? Playing board and card games as a family, or doing puzzles and parlor games like charades, are a great way to have fun and hang out together.

TAKE FIVE PLAYTIME

Make time in your day to be in nature with your children.

- Lie on the grass and watch the clouds, and see what shapes you can make from them.

- Inspect the petals on a flower up close.

- Watch the frenetic activity of ants as they busy themselves finding food.

- Make snow angels on the ground.

- Jump in puddles and kick your way through piles of leaves in the fall.

- Paddle in streams.

Be in nature with a childlike curiosity and allow your child to share the joy of experiencing things as if for the first time.

Making Time (For Them and You)

3 DEVELOPING RELATIONSHIPS

Let's get one thing straight. You cannot spoil a child by giving him too much love, attention, physical affection, or emotional connection. These are the strong foundations on which your children will build their resilience, sense of self-esteem, and ability to face whatever the world throws at them. Perversely, a strong emotional and relational bond with you will help your child to become more independent and confident.

A strong connection with your children means being there for them to meet their needs or if they are suffering emotionally, but it does not mean shielding them from all adversity, struggles, and sadness. All children need to learn the skills to deal with difficulties, knowing they have your support. Overindulgence, setting no boundaries, giving your children the sense that all of their whims and desires will be met, is what is commonly called spoiling and is definitely damaging. It is not what building strong bonds is all about.

Making Strong Bonds with Your Child

In order to foster a strong connection with your children, you need to spend time with them. Yes, that hoary old chestnut . . . But bonds cannot be made if you are always at work or they are always in organized activities.

First and foremost, to establish strong bonds, your children need to know they can count on you to meet their needs. Trust is paramount to a strong connection—so that's turning up to sports day if you say you'll be there, picking them up from clubs on time, recognizing when they are feeling below par and being understanding about it.

This trust is built through everyday family life—the mundane and routine chores as well as the fun days and celebrations.

"WE CAN ONLY BE SAID TO BE ALIVE IN THOSE MOMENTS WHEN OUR HEARTS ARE CONSCIOUS OF OUR TREASURES."

—THORNTON WILDER

In the eyes of a young child, anything that takes your attention away is essentially a separation. And unfortunately, in our time-pressed lives, a certain amount of separation is inevitable. Too much time apart will corrode connection but the good news is that you can maintain good bonds if, when you physically reunite with your child, you reconnect emotionally as well. Be present, be mindful in the time you spend together, and your relationship will flourish.

Feeling Grateful

A great way to reinforce the bonds that bind your family is to do a daily gratitude practice altogether. It only takes a few moments each day—at the dinner table, on the school run, at bath time—to share something you are each grateful for. It's surprising how much it makes you appreciate what you have and how good it makes you feel.

TAKE FIVE · MINDFUL CONNECTION

Together with your children, choose favorite family photos to print, or sketch pictures of fond memories. Stick them onto a board to form a happiness collage, and position it somewhere where the family will frequently see it—for example, above the dinner table, in the kids' bedrooms, or even in the bathroom.

Each time your children see the board, they will be reminded of happy family times and the bonds that you share will be reinforced.

Update it and add to it often, and ask them about the memories it prompts. Good memories can be the cement of good connections.

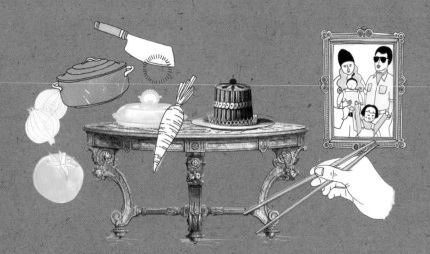

"OUR DOPAMINE
OUTPUT INCREASES NOT ONLY
WHEN WE EXPERIENCE SOMETHING
PLEASURABLE THE FIRST TIME, BUT
AGAIN WHEN WE REMEMBER IT . . .
[BY REMINISCING] WE AND OUR
CHILDREN CAN ENJOY MORE OF
WHAT WE ALREADY HAVE."

—GOLDIE HAWN, *10 MINDFUL MINUTES* (2012)

RECONNECTING

If you have a difficult relationship with your child and you feel the bond is damaged in some way, don't despair. The closeness that you felt to your child when she was younger can be reestablished with some effort, and it is never too late to reconnect to your child. Through mindfulness practice, you will have the emotional awareness to reach out to your child, to find creative ways to make connections again on a daily basis, and to pay attention to how your child is responding so that you can heal your bond.

Good Communication

One of the best ways to nurture good connections within the family
is to make sure you have good communications among all the members.
And for that to happen, each member of the family must feel safe to speak
up without danger of being criticized, blamed, or disregarded. Every
member of the family must feel able to speak their truth, and trust that
their view or perspective will be listened to and respected.

The Importance of Attunement

Attunement—the ability to read and respond to the
communicated needs of your child—has been found to be an
important factor in young children's development. A study by the
Society for Research in Child Development found that mothers
who spent lots of time exchanging back-and-forth eye contact,
gestures, and responsive language with their infants helped to
develop the child's linguistic and attachment skills. Research by
the UK's National Childbirth Trust also found that reciprocal
communication in a child's first two years influenced language
acquisition and later school performance.

> "RESPECTFUL COMMUNICATION UNDER CONFLICT OR OPPOSITION IS AN ESSENTIAL AND TRULY AWE-INSPIRING ABILITY."
>
> —BRYANT MCGILL, HUMAN-POTENTIAL THOUGHT LEADER

That doesn't mean that, as parents, you relinquish the role of being in charge. It simply means that everyone in the family has the freedom to have their say and that their voices will be heard, even though you always have the casting vote. In order for each member of the family to be able to communicate effectively and freely, you must first know what you feel and thus what you need to say. If you grew up in an emotionally intelligent, mindful family home, where you were encouraged to talk about how things made you feel, this will come naturally. For those who grew up in a home environment where it didn't feel safe to speak your truth, then you may find mindful communication within your own nuclear family hard. This is where meditation and daily mindfulness practices will help you to identify old habits and underlying fears that are being perpetuated in your new family life. Taking time to check in with how you are feeling about certain situations will help to bring you greater clarity and help you to communicate your feelings more clearly with the rest of the family.

TAKE FIVE · COMMUNICATING MINDFULLY

Here are a few exercises that can help you to communicate effectively, respectfully, and in a spirit of cooperation with your family.

• Make sure you communicate in the first person. So, for example: "I feel irritated when you leave wet towels on your bedroom floor. It feels disrespectful and it flouts what we agreed." This sort of language may feel alien to you at first, but by communicating using "I" statements, you are taking responsibility for your own feelings, you are clearly explaining the situation without blame, and you are identifying for your child (and perhaps yourself) what the nub of the problem is. In this way you honor yourself, show respect for your child, and communicate clearly. Better still, repeated use of this form of communication results in better understanding and it gets the job done.

• When you find yourself reacting to a situation and you don't know why, you often communicate the wrong messages. Take a moment to look at the long-held belief behind your reaction and pretend you believe the exact opposite. Make a mental note of how you feel and what thoughts come to mind.

• Help your children to recognize how they are feeling using an analogy of the weather, such as "I feel sunny," or "I feel stormy." It allows them to label their present state without being too attached to the emotion they are experiencing; i.e. "I am not the tsunami but I recognize that a huge wave is washing over me."

• Acknowledge or validate the feelings of all participants in the conversation, even if you don't agree with them. In this way, every member of the family's perspective is respected, even though this doesn't necessarily make them right. By showing that you have heard what they are saying and understand it, you are validating their feelings. If you start this practice when they are young, it becomes so much easier to make sure you are both understood once they are teenagers and situations become heated.

4 DEALING WITH EMOTIONS

Just like adults, children can be surprised and confused by their feelings and emotions. Often they do not recognize exactly what they are feeling and, even if they do, they have no idea how to cope. Your role is to teach your children how to be present with their feelings, to notice them and give them attention but not to confuse what they are feeling with who they are. For example, "I am not a scaredy-cat, I just feel anxious about being in the dark."

It is vital that you do not give your child the impression that some feelings are acceptable and others—namely "negative feelings"—are not. Once your children realize that feelings are just that—you have them, but you are not what you are feeling, and the feeling will pass—then they soon learn that no feelings need to be repressed, ignored, changed, or even acted on. By simply teaching your child to allow, feel, and accept feelings, you are giving strategies to deal with any emotion that may arise.

A Mindful Approach to Anger

While we need to give our children an understanding that all feelings
are OK, equally we need them to understand that not all reactions to
those feelings are acceptable. Anger expressed as lashing out verbally or
physically is a prime example of this. It can be quite difficult to convey
to your child the fact that anger in itself is not a "bad emotion"—after all,
we can't help how we feel—but it is how we choose to react to and
express the anger that is important.

Obviously, you will want to address unwanted behavior once a
situation has calmed down, but when your child is in the heat of the
moment and anger consumes her, she needs your help. Firstly, you need to
connect with your child, who is probably feeling frightened by the strength
of the emotion and out of control. Once you have been able to soothe,
comfort, and calm your child, she will then be able to hear what you have
to say—and will move from a reactive situation to a receptive state, where
your words will be heard and your child can learn. At this point, once you
have her attention, when you talk about the implications of her angry
actions, the message is heard and understood.

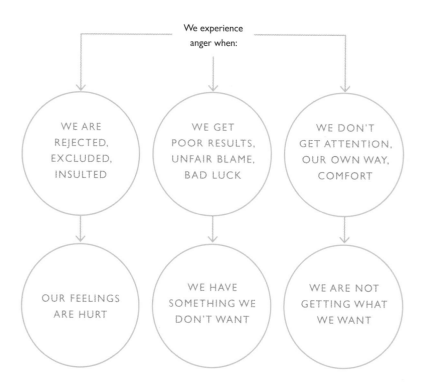

We experience anger when:

- WE ARE REJECTED, EXCLUDED, INSULTED
- WE GET POOR RESULTS, UNFAIR BLAME, BAD LUCK
- WE DON'T GET ATTENTION, OUR OWN WAY, COMFORT

- OUR FEELINGS ARE HURT
- WE HAVE SOMETHING WE DON'T WANT
- WE ARE NOT GETTING WHAT WE WANT

By using an empathetic approach and connecting first, your child feels understood, or "felt," and so better able to listen without drama and without the situation escalating still further—as it might if you'd reacted in an angry fashion yourself. By responding in a calm and loving way, you are demonstrating to your child that there are other ways to interact with people when you are feeling angry and upset.

Dealing with Emotions

TAKE FIVE

HANDLING EMOTIONS MINDFULLY

Next time your child is swept up in a strong emotion, ask him to notice where he is feeling it in his body and how it feels. Ask him to stay with it a while and to notice how the feeling in the body changes.

Have a paper and crayons or coloring pencils ready. Now, ask your child to remember those feelings and to draw them, or to put them into words: "I feel happy and this is how it looks . . ." You can substitute any emotion here, from anger and pain to love. With younger children, they may prefer to close their eyes and describe the emotion and how it feels to you.

By practicing this exercise, your child becomes able to recognize what a particular feeling—sadness, fear, frustration—feels like, and he becomes better able to spot it early and direct his attention to it, without it taking grip. He learns that strong emotions will not defeat him.

Giving your children a calm and sympathetic response to their overwhelming feelings, and helping them to realize that the feeling will pass, is hugely reassuring. For some children, it is enough for them to know that you are listening, that they are heard, and that you are not judging them when their feelings threaten to get the better of them. For others, being given a comforting hug or holding their hand is all it takes.

The Art of Empathy

Children learn empathy through interacting with parents and others, face to face. It is through eye contact and interaction with others that it begins to dawn on young children that another person has feelings. You can build on this first insight, fostering empathy by playing empathic and compassionate games, and by encouraging increased face-to-face interactions.

Through mindful practices and attention, your children become more attuned to observing details and focusing their attention, and this is useful when developing the skills of empathy. In the same way, when children are encouraged to practice acts of kindness, their compassion grows and they are better equipped to recognize when people are in need.

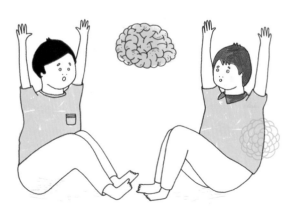

TAKE FIVE | EMPATHY EXERCISES

EMPATHY WITH OTHERS

• When you are reading a story with your child, get him to try to label the emotions of the characters at a particular juncture of the story.

• Similarly, when watching a DVD, pause the movie or show and ask your child to tell you what emotion that character is feeling from their facial expressions and body language.

• You can even get your child to draw happy, sad, angry, or embarrassed faces as a bit of fun.

KINDNESS GAME

Encourage each member of the family to give compliments—not simply, "I like your new dress," but meaningful compliments that reflect on the person's behavior. For example, "I am so pleased when you have a drink and biscuit waiting for me after gymnastics." Over dinner, you can discuss the compliments that each member has given, and the recipient's response.

MIRRORING GAME

Get two children to sit facing each other, looking into each other's eyes. One player is the leader and the other player is the "mirror." The leader then pulls facial expressions to convey certain emotions, and the mirror has to copy those expressions and name the emotions. Take it in turns. You can also extend the game to include physical movements.

Nonjudgmental Parenting

As we have seen, the essence of mindfulness is being in the present and paying attention nonjudgmentally. However, the nonjudging part of mindfulness is often the hardest to master, not only when looking at our own behavior and experiences but also those of our children. As a result of our own past experiences and upbringing, we have formed strong opinions, which, in reality, are simply thoughts. Yet, we use these opinions (thoughts) to form judgments—good or bad, right or wrong—on what is appropriate behavior from our children.

When faced with your child's strong emotions, it's important to be aware that your mind is constantly judging, based on your preformed opinions, and to try and suspend that judgment. Try to get your mind simply to observe what is actually happening and note the subtleties of each individual event. This will help you to stop letting your bias and prejudice confirm what you think you already know about your child's behavior. Hold

Nonjudging Exercise

You are using nonjudgmental parenting skills with your child but are you using nonjudgment on yourself as a parent? It is human nature to focus on the things that you feel you have done wrong as a parent, but how often do you focus on the things that you have done well? With as much self-compassion and generosity as you can muster, give thought and consideration to what you have done right as a parent recently and be pleased with yourself.

> "IF YOU JUDGE PEOPLE, YOU HAVE NO TIME TO LOVE THEM."
>
> **—MOTHER TERESA**

your preconceptions in awareness and question just how relevant or truthful they might be on each occasion.

In this way, you can use mindfulness and discernment to connect with your child. Suspending judgment and cultivating discernment will help you to avoid knee-jerk reactions; you will escape the limited way of seeing your child that is solely based on your own fears and mindset.

5 ENCOURAGING POSITIVE BEHAVIOR

Mindful parents who want to raise cooperative and self-disciplined children need to focus on connection and coaching as opposed to control and punishment—and this takes a lot of self-awareness. All the research shows that punishment doesn't work; in fact, it erodes your relationship with your child. Instead, it is the loving connection with your children and the help that you give them in learning to handle their emotions (see Chapter Four) that makes them want to behave as you would like.

In mindful parenting, there is no need to threaten or punish. When you are frightened or angry, or simply wanting to stop misbehavior in the moment, you may revert to punishment rather than teaching. However, with practice, you can encourage positive behavior purely by being calm and in the moment, by taking a breath, and responding to your child with loving guidance.

A Good Start in Life

In 1990, the Search Institute in California released a framework of
40 "Developmental Assets," which identifies a set of skills, experiences,
relationships, and behaviors that enable children to develop into successful
and contributing adults.

Data collected from Search Institute surveys of more than 5 million
children and youths from all backgrounds and situations has consistently
demonstrated that the more Developmental Assets young people acquire,
the better their chances of succeeding in school and becoming happy,
healthy, contributing members of their communities and society.

The categories on the list of assets are:

• External Assets—support, empowerment, boundaries and expectations,
  and constructive use of time.

• Internal Assets—commitments to learning, positive values, social
  competencies, and positive identity.

You can download the age-appropriate lists, which cover children of three
up to teens, from the Search Institute website (search-institute.org).

LOVING KINDNESS MEDITATION

It is important to model positive behavior while your children are young. By practicing *metta* (loving kindness) you are exhibiting good behavior to your child while also taking a good step toward improving your own behavior, and you may find you are better able to deal with your child's misbehavior with ease and lightness.

Sit quietly for five minutes and visualize your emotional heart located in your chest. Bring to mind the intention that you wish to increase self-compassion and love for others. You may like to picture this compassion as a seed that you tend and which grows as you continue your practice. Meditate on the phrase, "I live with kindness and at ease." Expand this to include your family members: "May you [name] live with kindness and at ease."

"I LIVE WITH KINDNESS AND AT EASE."

"MAY YOU LIVE WITH KINDNESS AND AT EASE."

Setting Limits

Critics often confuse mindful parenting with permissive parenting, but although both rely heavily on respect and empathy in relationships with children, the mindful parent is also prepared to offer clear limits and structure. Mindful parents have age-appropriate expectations of their children but are heavily involved, so that a child is supported when facing life's difficulties. Mindful parents may even be demanding, but they offer their children lots of love and support on the way to meeting these high expectations. They have a healthy and trusting connection with their children, which helps the children come to terms with limits that may not feel fair, or that they may not like.

Setting healthy and necessary limits for your kids, which can be whatever you judge to be right for your family—perhaps they center on television and social networking, junk foods, or disrespectful and violent behavior—teaches your children that there are limits to their ability to change certain situations, and that their parents are always a reliable and sympathetic presence.

By establishing limits from a young age around family issues such as bedtimes, manners, or household chores, your children will develop their own ability to exercise self-awareness and self-protection, so that they make healthier choices and are better able to set their own boundaries.

Expectations with Support

The expectations you have of your children are age-appropriate but they lay the foundations for future behavior as your children grow and develop. So, you might introduce the idea of an expectation that your child helps with tidying her room at the age of three, for example. Clearly, your child will need your help to tidy up at that age, and initially you will need to be involved and supportive every time the room-tidying chore comes round. However, within a few years, and if you are persistent in the practice, your child will be tidying her bedroom on her own each week, with only the gentlest of reminders.

Further Down the Line

As your children grow and mature, so you may want to review your limits and evaluate which ones still serve them well. It is a fine line between being too firm so they start to lie or withdraw, and too relaxed, which exposes them to the potentially negative influences of peer or societal pressure. Your limit setting will shift and change in response to each different child, different ages, and different situations, but as long as you keep reassessing your judgment from the perspective of what is right for each child, then you are honoring a mindful approach.

Most importantly, if your children know intuitively that your limits come from a place of care and concern and they feel connected to you and the family, then their responses are more likely to be positive (even though they may still tell you just how furious they feel about any limits imposed on their behavior).

Empowerment

One of the factors the Search Institute found to promote positive behavior and reduce high-risk behavior in later life (see page 60) is the external asset of empowerment, which relies heavily on empathic behavior and interconnectedness. So, it is important that young kids feel welcomed and included in community life and that as they get older, they feel valued and appreciated by the adults in the community.

Another quality to foster in your kids to empower them is service to others. At a young age this could mean encouraging your child to do kind and caring actions for other members of the immediate and extended family. By the time your child is eight, you could think about giving him the opportunity to help others in the community and, when he is in his teens, volunteering in the community on a regular basis is of great benefit. You can give your children the confidence to go out and help others and to show empathic behavior by making sure they feel safe and valued, not only at home but also in the community.

HELPING OTHERS → LEARNING EMPATHY → FEELING WELCOMED AND VALUED

Consequences and Taking Responsibility

Natural consequences of your child's actions can be an excellent teacher, but consequences should not be confused with punishment. If your child forgets to take her hooded raincoat for the school trip and is going to get wet, she may or may not learn the lesson and remember it next time. If she asks you to bring it to school before the bus leaves, your response is crucial to the lesson of consequences. You may dash in with the coat once but if you do so repeatedly, the consequences of her actions will be lost on her. If you choose to respond with a refusal delivered in a "serves you right" tone, then she may remember the coat next time but she will also gather that you don't care about her and potentially cooperate less at home—the consequences of her actions have become a punishment.

You compound the negative message still further if you add that she's forgotten her coat because she's scatterbrained and you are always the one who has to pick up the pieces. On top of showing a lack of care, this conveys the message that she's forgetful and a burden to you.

An alternative and more effective response would be to say that you can't come in on this occasion because you have a prior commitment you can't drop, but you hope she doesn't get too wet and you'll run her a bath later so she can have a hot soak when she gets home. Your child may well remember the lesson of the consequences of forgetting her coat in future, but your response also means that she still feels cared about and her self-image remains undented.

So, letting your children experience the consequences of their actions and decisions can work as long as it is not a consequence that you, as the parent, have contrived to use as a form of discipline.

MINDFUL RESPONSIBILITY

We don't want to teach our children that they should never make mistakes but we do want them to know that they should take responsibility for their actions and emotions and make right what is wrong. The best way for them to understand and learn this tricky mindfulness practice is by modeling it yourself. Your children are more likely to accept responsibility for a mistake if they feel safe and loved and that they won't be shamed and blamed.

When your child breaks something through rough play or refuses to get dressed so you are running late for work, you probably feel stressed and angry. In that moment, look below the surface of your reaction. Why does it cause you so much distress? Could it be that you are frustrated because your child is interfering with the smooth running of your life? Are you worried that being late will make you look ridiculous in the eyes of your co-workers? Do you feel out of control?

When something stressful happens, instead of reacting on impulse remember to take four steps:

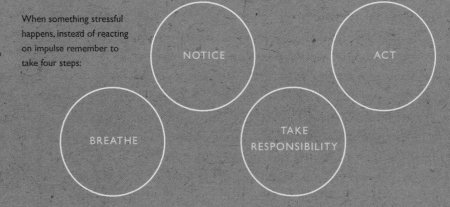

Sharing Moments

When our son hit a golf ball through our neighbor's greenhouse, we acknowledged that he had not done so on purpose, but told him that he had to make amends. He visited Roy to apologize and offered to pay. Shrewdly, Roy would accept no payment but asked our son to help him in his workshop in reparation. A wonderful friendship blossomed from those "repayment" sessions and my son learned woodwork!

Next time your child does something that makes you feel mad, take a moment to breathe and to notice your own reaction. Observe your feelings of impatience, frustration, stress, vulnerability, or lack of control, and take responsibility for them. Calmly give your child the tools to rectify his actions—a cloth to wipe the yogurt off the walls, for example.

In this way, you are showing your children how to take responsibility for your reactions without putting your feelings of frustration on them, or shaming and blaming them. You are effectively modeling how to take responsibility for your own actions, feelings, and reactions.

6 NURTURING SELF-ESTEEM

How is it that one of your children is animal mad and another simply wants to spend all her time dancing? Children are predisposed to certain passions and it is up to you to help them discover this passion or purpose, whatever it may be. Mindful parenting means being open to all possibilities, even if it means your children drift from one topic or pastime to another until they find what brings them joy. Most importantly, you must avoid the temptation to push them in a specific direction that holds no appeal for them simply because it is something that you like or approve of for them. Through encouraging your children to find their own passions—what excites them and what they will almost certainly be good at—you are helping to bolster their sense of self and their uniqueness.

Exploring Passions and Strengths

Fostering children's curiosity about their passions involves plenty of unstructured free time and the chance to meet a wide variety of people, as well as having a breadth of different experiences. Too much structured activity and an over-stuffed schedule cheat your children of the chance to explore the ideas and things that enliven them. This zest for life will be instilled in your children from the earliest age if they see you using your spare time doing what you love. You are modeling the importance of learning and exploring in your life. How wonderful to engender that gift in your children. Perhaps you have yet to find what brings you joy yourself—carve out some time for yourself to explore anything that catches your eye or piques your curiosity. This will tell you what your heart truly desires.

If you are able to incorporate purpose and passion in your own life, and encourage your children to do so too, you will help to protect them from future apathy and can share the joy that passion brings to life.

YOUR KIDS WILL REMAIN MOTIVATED AND COMMITTED TO ACTIVITIES WHEN PURSUING PASSIONS THAT ARE IMPORTANT TO THEM RATHER THAN GOALS GENERATED BY YOU.

TAKE FIVE FOLLOWING YOUR PASSION

Like most parents, you probably feel that you do not have enough time to pursue your own hobbies and interests. Take five minutes to reflect on and record what you would do purely for pleasure if you had the time. Think about when you last spent time engaged in an activity you love, and then list what prevents you from pursuing it. Not just the trite "not enough time" answer—go deeper. In reality, could you claw back odd free moments to get into the garden, watch the stars, or play the guitar?

Finally, play with the idea of how you might practically reintroduce this activity into your family life. When would be the best day to find some time? Could the children accompany you, or is there someone who might mind them for you? Visualize how this might become a tangible possibility, to reconnect to your passion and nourish your soul.

Honing Skills and Gifts

Psychiatrists suggest that your child's future happiness has less to do with the traditional definitions of success (i.e. academic achievement, good job, high standard of living) and more to do with being able to explore his unique abilities and skills, being allowed to hone them, and to share them in the wider world.

By encouraging your child to do the activities he loves and to pursue his goals with passion and commitment, wholeheartedly, you are opening him up to the wonderful gifts of achievement and fulfillment—and with these come happiness and self-esteem. When your child is so totally absorbed and focused on what he is doing that time is forgotten, this is akin to what scientists call being in the flow, sportsmen call being in the zone, and aesthetes call being in bliss or in joy.

Your unconditional love is the first step on the road to nurturing self-esteem in your children. The next step is built on accomplishments. If they can master tasks, skills, and challenges as they grow up, through practice, training, and perseverance, so their self-esteem will blossom and they will feel able to share and showcase their talents and make their dreams an actuality.

Once this approach to experiences and goals has been learned, it will stand your children in good stead for the future and for all the ambitions that follow. Your kids will be well equipped to take joy in pursuing hobbies, sport, creativity, and work—whether they are viewed by others as having succeeded or not—because they know how to enjoy the process of finessing their natural talents in order to reach the goal. It is the journey rather than the arrival that counts.

Ways to Foster Mastery

- Let your kids learn by experimenting—if you always show them how, they will not develop an inquiring mind or self-reliance.

- Allow your children to keep control—so if a task looks to be beyond their ability, don't rush in and take over. Rather, make useful suggestions, give encouragement, and help only when asked. If you always intervene to show them how, or to do it for them, you give them the message that they are not capable.

- Appreciate your children at every stage of their development—it's such a temptation to direct and rescue, when it is better to allow your kids to discover and explore at their own pace according to their own unique nature.

- Reinforce the value of exploring and learning, over the merits of achievement—this helps your children to keep motivated to practice something in order to eventually master it.

- Praise efforts, not results—better to say, "You've worked really hard on that painting. I'm so impressed with you," rather than "That's a lovely painting." In this way, you encourage your child to keep trying, and emphasize the message that hard work pays off.

- Model self-talk—let your children see you using mantras such as "I can do it, I can do it," when you are struggling to achieve something. They will then be able to use the same self-encouragement and motivation as self-critical thoughts in their heads kick in, when faced with difficulty or disappointment in a task.

- Support your children's interests—if your kids' goals are generated by you, how can you expect them to be motivated to pursue them? Allow your children to discover their own interests and passions through trial and error and exploration. Of course these will change (too frequently to the minds of many parents), but try to respect each new exploration.

Building Resilience

One of the greatest qualities you can foster in your child through mindful parenting is resilience—namely, the ability to adapt well to adversity, trauma, tragedy, threats, or even significant sources of tension—as it is resilience that helps your children manage stress and feelings of anxiety and uncertainty.

Take some time to contemplate how you can implement the following techniques into your parenting approach, in order to help your child develop resilience. Reflect on a situation in the past where these techniques might have been helpful in dealing with a specific circumstance, and think about how you might interact differently with your child, given the same set of circumstances again. Here are the tips to bear in mind when opportunities present themselves to help your kids deal with difficulties and adversity:

> "RESILIENCE IS BASED ON COMPASSION FOR OURSELVES AS WELL AS COMPASSION FOR OTHERS."
>
> —SHARON SALZBERG, AUTHOR AND MEDITATION TEACHER

- Encourage your children to build connections and friendships by empathizing with and helping others. Connecting with people provides social support and strengthens resilience.

- Try to make sure your children's goals are realistic. You don't want to find yourself in the position of having to choose between letting your child fail or rescuing her and potentially disempowering her in the process.

- Help your children to understand that it is during the tough times and the failures that you learn the most about yourself. Help them to notice that they can handle whatever they are facing, and that they now have the skills and experience to avoid failing next time.

- Make sure your children can count on you to support and empathize when they experience difficulty, disappointment, and frustration. Knowing you will be there for them, to connect and care, will give your children the confidence to risk failure and disappointment in the certain knowledge that they will survive it—and will, in fact, build resilience.

Bear in mind that developing resilience is a personal journey. What works for one child might not work for another, so use your knowledge of your own children to guide them on their journey.

7 THE BREATH OF LIFE

Focusing on your breath is one of the most common practices in mindfulness and it is an essential tool for mindful parenting. When a challenging situation with your child is escalating and you can feel your frustration or anger rising, taking a few moments to focus on your breath helps to center you and to give you clarity and calmness in the moment, rather than the knee-jerk flight, fight, or freeze reaction produced by the stress response in the body. Now you become present to your children again and it's easier to reflect on what's going on for them, how they might be feeling, and how best to respond.

With practice, you will be able to apply mindful breath awareness to any situation that arises in your life, from the mundane to the extreme. And you can teach your children to use mindful breathing to good effect in their lives too.

Understanding the Breath

When you are stressed, the limbic system (your survival system) in the brain kicks in. The amygdala responds to unfamiliar, dangerous, emotional, thrilling, or painful situations by triggering the fight, flight, or freeze response, flooding your body with stress hormones and neurochemicals that put you in an emergency state of high alert.

This was useful in our caveman days, but less useful now when stress is part of most parents' everyday lives. As a result, without realizing it, you probably spend a lot of time with your body in survival mode—a faster heart rate, blood pressure raised, digestive system malfunctioning. Spend too long with chronic stress, and the survival mode setting for your body becomes the norm—and with it all the serious health implications for your body and your mind.

You will recognize many of the myriad triggers for stress in adult lives, such as paper jams in the printer, running late, car breakdowns, canceled trains, calls from the school, losing things, multitasking, and many others. The triggers for children are different, as we saw in Chapter One, but the fight, flight, or freeze response is just the same. And sadly, the effects of chronic cumulative stress are just as destructive.

"YOU CAN'T 'TAKE' A BREATH, YOUR BREATH IS GIVEN TO YOU."

—SHIVA REA, YOGA TEACHER

Explaining to your children that the stress response causes them to have a physiological reaction that can make them prone to behavior such as aggression, lashing out, screaming, crying, and other overreactions—but that you can use your breath to calm yourself and to refocus whenever you need—gives them a great tool for life. Knowing that taking a few slow, deep breaths will help them to feel they have some control in challenging situations, and when they're feeling upset or "out of control," is comforting for children of all ages.

TAKE FIVE · OBSERVING YOUR BREATH

Normally your breathing is shallow, using just the top part of the lungs, especially if you work at a desk. This mindful breathing exercise focuses your mind (strengthening your attention), energizes the body as you fill your lungs, then relaxes the body as you breathe out.

- Find a quiet place where you can comfortably sit upright and where you will not be disturbed.

- Start by taking your mind to how your body "feels." Any tensions? Relax your body, especially the muscles in your abdomen and belly.

- Take your attention to your breath—feel the chest and belly rise on the in-breath and fall on the out-breath.

- Lengthen the in-breath and the out-breath and observe them.

- If your mind wanders, that's OK. Gently bring it back to your breath without judgment.

- Allow your breath to settle back into its natural rhythm and bring yourself back to the room.

MINDFUL BREATHING FOR CHILDREN

- Ask your children to sit comfortably with you and to close their eyes.

- If they prefer, they can focus on an object such as a flower, a picture, or even their hands in their laps.

- Ask them to imagine the air coming in through their nose and flooding through their body, then to see it leaving on the out-breath. Can they feel their tummy rise and fall with the breath?

- Explain that outside noises and interruptions might distract them, and that's OK—they should just bring their attention back to their breath each time. The same applies if they feel the need to fidget or scratch an itch.

- Start with just a few moments for younger children, and build up to five minutes.

- At the end, discuss with your children how it felt and talk about ways they can use slow, deep breaths to calm themselves when they are tense or they are in tricky situations.

RECOGNIZING THE SIGNS

With regular practice, mindful breathing can train your brain to focus on the breath in response to stress, so that you then respond to stress mindfully and reflectively, rather than on impulse or with anger or panic.

But first you and your child need to recognize what happens to the breath when you are stressed or anxious. The following exercise is great for that.

Next time you watch a scary movie or a cartoon thriller together as a family, wait for a high-drama moment to pass and then ask your children if they noticed what happened to their breath in the heat of that moment. "Did you hold your breath while you were hiding behind the cushion? Was your breathing very shallow or restrained as the tension mounted? What do you think that means?"

If your children get used to noticing their breath, especially at tense or scary moments, they will come to recognize that they take quick, shallow breaths when they become tense. Next time a film is scary, perhaps they will be able to breathe more deeply during particularly tense scenes, and then they can come to recognize how deep breaths can relax them.

THREE-PART BREATH (*DIRGA PRANAYAMA*)

This is an excellent yogic breathing exercise that can be practiced sitting in the lotus position or cross-legged, or lying down in *shavasana* (the corpse pose). It really helps you to focus on the present moment and to get in touch with the sensations in your physical body.

- Start by drawing your attention to your natural breathing.

- Now deepen your breathing.

- Breathe into your belly, then let the in-breath expand your ribs and finally the upper chest all the way up to the collarbone.

- At the top of your in-breath, pause a moment in the still point.

- Then exhale fully, letting the air go first from the upper chest, then from the rib cage, and finally from the belly.

- At the bottom of the breath, when there is no more air left, pause momentarily in the still point before repeating the round of breathing another nine or ten times.

After the Practice

After sharing a mindful breathing session with your children, give them a chance to share their experiences with you. Even if it's simply to tell you that they had difficulty staying focused, you can explain that we all find these practices easier on some days than others and to be patient (a hard concept for children who are used to a world of instant gratification).

LISTEN OPENLY AND WITHOUT JUDGMENT.

For those who report any calm feelings they may have experienced, this can lead into a discussion on how mindful breathing could be used elsewhere, whether it's when they are feeling nervous about a school test or when they are being bugged by a younger sibling.

Listen openly and without judgment to what they report. Children also enjoy hearing about your experience of the practice as this makes it feel more of a shared experience. And don't forget to tell them how much you enjoyed doing this practice together—it all helps to cement that mindful connection.

Like many parents, I used to tell my children to "calm down" when they were getting overexcited. It wasn't until we started practicing mindful breathing as a family that my nine-year-old son confessed he'd never understood what I'd meant by "calm down." He didn't know how, until we introduced mindful breathing as a response to something difficult or daunting.

Now I am so accustomed to mindful breathing that I find myself practicing it while sitting in a traffic jam, in the supermarket checkout line, or while on the train. In fact, just about anywhere. Yet, it still remains a particular treat for me to set aside special time and space to tune in to my breath. So, I will often take a mini-break from my desk to sit in my meditation chair with a candle lit and to enjoy a few precious minutes of mindful breathing practice.

8 THE POWER OF SLEEP

Sleep deprivation is all part of being the parent of young children. As they get older, the interrupted nights may pass, but the stress of modern living means that millions of parents report that thinking or worrying about things keeps them awake at night. Others say that they fall asleep instantly, but then they awake in the middle of the night and cannot get back to sleep.

Sleep problems in children are a relatively new phenomenon, occurring largely as a result of overscheduled, over-pressurized lives, and also because of exposure to electronic devices and stimulating media at bedtime and in children's bedrooms.

Sleep is important for us all but particularly for kids, as it is during sleep that their learning pathways are strengthened. Children who do not get enough sleep have problems with attention, hyperactivity, and mood swings, and underperform at school, or suffer from anxiety and depression.

Good Sleep Routines

Establishing good sleep habits in young children will stand them in good stead for the rest of their lives. Young children dislike bedtime because it means being separated from their parents and being alone in the dark, but if you have a loving, supportive bedtime ritual that you use consistently, bedtime becomes much easier for you and your child.

The process is made more difficult if you and your child are both tired and wound up before the ritual starts, so try to limit screen time and stimulating play leading up to the tidying-up, bath-time, and story-time routine. Devote your time exclusively to your children at bedtime so that they get the connection, love, and nurture they need before falling asleep. That means leaving the phone and emails to one side, and making time

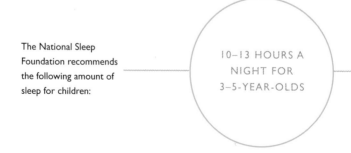

The National Sleep Foundation recommends the following amount of sleep for children:

10–13 HOURS A NIGHT FOR 3–5-YEAR-OLDS

for snuggles. Remember to stay calm and unflustered yourself—even if you are desperate to get back downstairs for a favorite TV show or a glass of wine. Getting angry at bedtime will only exacerbate your child's separation anxiety and make things harder.

Preempt the inevitable procrastination and power struggles by offering your child choices (both of which suit you), such as, "Do you want to wear the pink or the yellow nightdress?" This helps to empower your child during her bedtime rituals. Reading books, telling stories, cuddling, and talking is invaluable quality face-to-face time that you may not get at any other time during the day, so be present and enjoy it.

Finally, it helps to share mindful relaxation exercises with your children, so that they can fully relax and fall asleep each night. These skills will reap lifelong benefits. You can use them at bedtime, too.

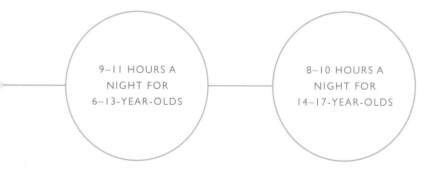

9–11 HOURS A
NIGHT FOR
6–13-YEAR-OLDS

8–10 HOURS A
NIGHT FOR
14–17-YEAR-OLDS

TAKE FIVE · GRATITUDE PRACTICE

This is an excellent mindful practice at bedtime for all ages.
It is part of my nightly routine and I'm not sure I could sleep
well without it. Cultivating gratitude for the big and small things
in life not only improves your physical and psychological health,
it also enhances empathy, reduces anger and aggression,
and improves mental agility and sleep!

As you lie in bed, give yourself a few minutes to relax your
muscles and get comfortable. Take a few deep breaths and then
turn your thoughts to the things that you are grateful for today
(and every day): family, friendship, a smile from a ticket collector,
the first flower of spring—you get the gist.

Silently give thanks for each thing, while calling on all of your
senses to feel the sensation of gratitude.

With a smile on your face, allow yourself to drift gently
off to sleep.

The Family Bed

The debate around whether children should be allowed to sleep in their parents' bed still rages, and it is a very personal decision. If you are persuaded by the benefits of having your infants in the bed with you—and it is certainly the norm in many Far Eastern countries, where it is felt that a parent's physical presence, closeness, and breathing at night is a comfort and reassurance—then there are safety precautions that you can adopt to make co-sleeping safer (see guidelines from the University of Notre Dame's Mother–Baby Behavioral Sleep Laboratory, at cosleeping.nd.edu/safe-co-sleeping-guidelines).

A good compromise can be having a cot set up in your bedroom. Your child gets the comfort of sleeping in the same room as you, but he also has the option of going to his own room when that feels right. You can also move your child to his own room after he is asleep if you want to be alone.

Fear and Sleep

Anxiety and separation fears are often the root cause of children's sleep issues. Mindful coaching to work through the fears can help your children overcome these issues.

Remember, it is entirely natural to get upset or frustrated when your child throws tantrums and struggles each night, especially when you're sleep-deprived yourself. So focus on staying calm and being patient when coaching your child to fall asleep alone.

After the bedtime routine, announce your intention to leave, reassuring your child that you know she can fall asleep by herself and that you will keep her safe. Attempt to leave the room but remain to comfort her if she panics and struggles. Once she has settled, promise to return if you are needed, and try again. Repeat as often as necessary.

This loving approach, whereby you announce your plan to leave and then help your children through their anxious reaction, helps them to deal with their fears and sleep through the night alone.

RESEARCH BY BOSTON'S BENSON-HENRY INSTITUTE FOR MIND BODY MEDICINE SHOWS THAT PRACTICING MINDFUL BREATHING CAN HELP PARENTS AND CHILDREN TO SLEEP BETTER AND RETURN TO SLEEP MORE EASILY IF THEY WAKE IN THE NIGHT.

YOGA MUSCLE RELAXATION

By tensing and releasing your muscles you learn what a relaxed state feels like, which helps you to get yourself into that relaxed state any time you choose. It is ideal for you or your children to practice in bed, to help you fall asleep.

- Take a few slow, deep breaths.

- Breathe in and tense your toes and feet for a few seconds (three to four seconds is fine), then exhale slowly and release the tension.

- Breathe in and tighten your lower leg muscles, hold for a few seconds and then relax again with the exhale of breath.

- Take a deep breath and tense your upper legs, hold, and then relax.

- Take a deep breath and tense your abdomen and lower back, hold for a few seconds, and then relax.

- Repeat with your chest and upper back.

- Repeat with your hands and lower arms, then upper arms, shoulders, and neck.

- Finally, tense your whole body, hold for a few seconds, and then slowly exhale while ensuring your whole body relaxes from the tension.

- Repeat this process again.

Dreamtime and Creativity

Artists have long known about the connection between dreams and creativity, but scientific research now points to the same link. Studies reported by the American Psychological Association found that imaginative people may have higher dream recall, and that the eccentric nature of dreams—with their colorful, nonjudgmental inferences—resembles the free-association (brainstorming-the-possibilities) aspect of the creative process that precedes creation.

The creation of connections between things that didn't seem connected before is something that you can do in the dreamworld, while your rational daytime mind sees these pieces of information as separate. Dreams seem bizarre because they don't make sense to the rational waking conscious mind, which tries to give them purpose, but the connections you make with the information you have can lead to nocturnal creativity and solutions. Sometimes, even if you don't recall your dream, you can wake up with the perfect solution to a problem or difficult situation. The answer came in your sleep because your mind was working to make different connections that resulted in a breakthrough.

To harness the wonderful creativity and solution-finding of dreams, it is worth keeping a notebook next to your bed and next to your children's beds. The immediate post-sleep, dreamlike mental state known as sleep inertia, or the hypnopompic state, allows you or your child to sprinkle your waking, conscious thoughts with a little creative magic from the dreamworld. If you wait until later in the day, the rational conscious mind has too strong a grip and you will discount the often inconsistent, outlandish, and inspired ideas and connections that your sleeping mind makes.

9 FOOD FOR THE SOUL

Childhood obesity is one of the most serious global public health challenges for the 21st century, according to the World Health Organization. When the body reacts to danger (real or perceived, grizzly bear or scary movie) it becomes flooded with stress hormones. The body thinks it needs extra food to fuel the fight-or-flight response and so we crave high-energy foods like sugar and carbohydrates. This stress response—together with loneliness—is the root cause of much of today's overeating.

As well as countering the hidden stresses in your family life using mindful techniques, you can also combat unhealthy eating habits by bringing mindfulness to the table. Food should be savored by both the mind and the body. You will be surprised how much better food tastes and how much calmer you feel when you bring curiosity and attention to the act of eating.

Savoring Your Food

Eating mindfully enhances your gratitude for, and enjoyment of, food and aids digestion—but interestingly, it can also help you and your family to eat less. Children have an insatiable appetite for facts and they will love to discover that it takes about 20 minutes for the brain to register the feeling of being full. As a result, you often continue to eat when you've really had enough. Slowing down your eating can combat this. Get them into the habit of assessing whether the third, fourth, or fifth mouthful tastes as good as the first few bites.

Tasting, savoring, and appreciating your food is a great part of sharing meals together. It also teaches your children to become aware of what they are eating, so that they recognize good nourishment and can take responsibility for eating nutritiously when they are older.

TAKE FIVE GLORIOUS FOOD FUN

A fun way to slow down the eating process, and to focus the attention on what and how you are eating, is to try eating a meal with your non-dominant hand or with chopsticks, if these are unfamiliar to you.

So, as a family, use the knife and fork the other way round or try eating spaghetti Bolognese with chopsticks in your non-dominant hand (your dominant hand is the one you use to write or hold a bat). Be warned, this can get extremely messy.

It's great fun and one of the rare occasions where the kids are on a level playing field with the adults—in fact, they may adjust more quickly to using the non-dominant hand than you! More importantly, it is a simple yet effective way to focus attention and awareness on nourishment in the present moment, without making it feel like a lecture or a chore.

TAKE FIVE — MINDFUL EATING

Rediscover the pleasure of savoring your food. Take a favorite snack or finger food—sweet or savory, it is entirely up to you. For the sake of this exercise, let's say you've chosen some cashew nuts.

Let's just imagine that you are seeing and tasting a cashew nut for the first time.

- Hold the nut in your hand and examine it closely, observing its texture, color, shape, and size.

- Feel it with your fingers—is it pitted or smooth?

- Smell it. What aroma do you get as you inhale?

- Don't worry too much if you feel a little self-conscious at first—that's natural. Simply return your awareness, without judgment, to observing the cashew nut.

- Rub the cashew nut between your fingers next to your ear. Does it make any sort of sound?

- First, gently touch the nut to your lips, without tasting it, just sensing it, before gently putting the nut into your mouth. Leave it on the tongue without chewing yet. What sensation do you have? Are you salivating? How powerful is the urge to bite?

- Finally, take a conscious bite into the cashew nut and observe the unlocked flavors.

- Slowly, chew the nut and notice how the flavor, texture, and consistency change.

- Your body will tell you when you are ready to swallow—notice this—and consciously swallow the mouthful of crushed nut, tasting and savoring it as it goes down. How does it feel?

It's not practical to apply this practice to every forkful of food you eat at mealtimes, but notice how much better the food tastes and how much calmer you feel when you bring curiosity and attention to the act of eating. You can also do this with your favorite drinks.

Try doing this exercise with your child and share your observations and reactions.

Family Mealtimes

There is no shortage of information about the value of feeding our children nutritious, healthy food. Yet, the actual mealtime itself should be of equal importance in mindful parenting. Make eating together as a family without distraction from televisions, phones, or gadgets a priority. Sitting around the table together, making sure every member of the family gets the chance to share his or her thoughts and feelings about the day, is a great opportunity to foster better bonds.

Sharing Moments

While raising our family, we purposely built rituals around food into our lives. So, we always have fish pie on Christmas Eve and each child gets to choose a favorite meal or restaurant on birthdays and special occasions. They also each get a caterpillar birthday cake every year (even in their twenties), and a chocolate orange in the Christmas stocking. Food is an easy way to build bonds and memories.

Building a Future

Research from the University of Minneapolis shows that children who regularly eat dinner with the family perform better at school; communicate better with their parents; eat more nutritiously; feel better about themselves; and are less likely to become depressed, drink or smoke while underage, be destructive, or run away from home. They are also more likely to be committed to learning, believe their parents are proud of them, and eat a better diet into adulthood.

Don't get fixated on table manners and how much your child is eating, or mealtimes will become a power struggle. If you engage the whole family in conversation, then they will eat the healthy food that you are serving.

Through mindful dinnertime conversations, where parents set the example of talking honestly about the good and bad of their day, children can open up about their own highs and lows without feeling scrutinized or criticized. They can hear and be heard, and this helps them to process the lessons and advice of all the family.

Nourishing Your Child

Providing and taking nourishment is one of the fundamental activities of family life. It takes an inordinate amount of time and thought but is usually paid scant moment-to-moment attention. Yet, it is through feeding (whether by bottle or breast) that a baby's first connections are formed. Your children's trust in you is founded upon the sustenance and comfort you provide as they grow. So offering them nutritious food will obviously improve their physical good growth, but food prepared with loving kindness guarantees satisfaction and pleasure every time.

SHARING MOMENTS

Cooking together promotes healthy eating and is a wonderful way to spend quality time with the kids. Every year, we used to have a week's holiday in a cottage. From the youngest age, each family member had a night where they chose and prepared a meal (obviously with help when they were smaller). Choosing and buying the ingredients, preparing them, then cooking and serving the meal brings mindful attention to the food we eat and has given our sons a skill for life. I had no fears for them in terms of eating well when they went off to college as a result.

TAKE FIVE GROW YOUR OWN

In these days of ready-meals and pre-packaged supermarket foods, it can be hard for children to make the connection between what they eat and how it is produced. Growing your own fruit and vegetables not only helps them to understand where food comes from but it also helps them to get excited about food and eating.

Why not try planting some easy-to-grow fruit and vegetables in the garden with your child? Get them involved in every step, from planting out to tending the seedlings and picking the crops. Imagine their delight if they can cook and serve a meal containing their own homegrown produce. If you don't have much space, you can grow herbs or salad vegetables in pots or take a trip to a "pick your own" farm. This conveys the same message about how food is grown, picked, and delivered to the shops. Plus it's fun!

10 THE GREAT OUTDOORS

The time that children spend playing in parks, woods, and fields has shrunk dramatically in recent years due to a shortage of green spaces, and a rise in digital technology and parental fears. According to a nationwide poll by The Nature Conservancy, only ten percent of American children say they spend time outdoors every day. This growing tendency toward sedentary and inactive lifestyles presents a danger to your children's health, as well as to their social development. Kids who play outdoors have been shown to be fitter, healthier, and more physically confident.

Although it is not always easy to build outdoor play and activity into your children's lives, when you allow them to explore the freedom and wonders of being outside, it opens up opportunities to foster resilience, to revel in nature and to build a personal connection to the environment that will last a lifetime.

The Joy of Being Outdoors

There are huge health benefits linked to giving children regular outdoor activity and exercise. It impacts their growth, increases their metabolic rates—so their bodies are better able to process food—and benefits sleep. Clean air and exercise may help to boost natural immunity to disease. Regular exposure to sunlight increases the body's production of Vitamin D naturally and efficiently. Vitamin D is vital for bone growth, and reports have suggested that healthy exposure is linked to a decreased risk of cancer and diabetes.

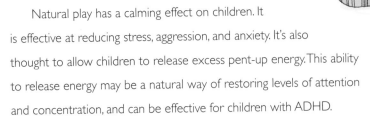

Natural play has a calming effect on children. It is effective at reducing stress, aggression, and anxiety. It's also thought to allow children to release excess pent-up energy. This ability to release energy may be a natural way of restoring levels of attention and concentration, and can be effective for children with ADHD.

In general, kids who play outdoors regularly have been assessed to have a greater general sense of happiness and well-being.

We have always spent a great deal of time as a family in the outdoors. Don't get me wrong; like most youngsters, our boys were happy to spend time on the PlayStation, but it took little encouragement to get them into the fresh air for an adventure. We did exciting activities with them, from canoeing to mountain biking, white-water rafting to abseiling. More importantly, we tried to inject fun into the more mundane—so a dog walk along the river became a marauding adventure, armed with sticks. We cooked bacon for breakfast over an open fire in the woods. We spent time in a yurt in the middle of the forest.

They had their fair share of bowling and cinema birthday parties, but the favorites were always when we set up camp in the back garden for a handful of kids and they would sit talking around the fire pit late into the night, watching marshmallows that fell into the fire turn into throbbing "alien brains."

TAKE FIVE

NATURE AS FAMILY

Give your children opportunities to be in nature and to witness its beauty in all its guises. Let them be part of it; teach your children to enjoy being outdoors so that they care about the future of our planet and all its wonderful inhabitants, not just humans.

HUG A TREE

"Tree hugger" is an insult that used to be leveled at hippies, but in terms of mindfulness activities, it doesn't come much better than exploring and feeling a tree.

Take time to be quiet in the woods and then ask each child to find a tree that really draws them, as if it is calling out to them.

Firstly, stand close to the tree and look at its bark—the pattern and the color. Slowly circle the tree. Is there more moss on one side than the other? Does the pattern of the bark vary?

Look up into the canopy and see the different colors of the leaves—and flowers if it is in bloom. Listen to the sound of the leaves rustling in the breeze; the sighing of the branches as they move.

Inhale deeply and smell the richness of the earth, the leaf mulch, or the dampness of the bark.

Mentally, ask the tree for permission before you lay your hands on the bark of the tree. Lean your back against it or sit against it . . . Be present with the tree and feel its power, energy, and wisdom.

STARGAZING

On a mild, clear night, take the family to a spot away from where there is too much light pollution.

Lay on the ground as if forming the spokes of a wheel, with your heads together at the hub and feet pointing out.

Allow your eyes to adjust and slow your breathing. Look up at the starry night sky and share what you see. Can you spot any constellations? Is that bright star a planet or a satellite? How does the sky change?

A variation on this game is to do the same during the day, and to observe the clouds. Notice how fast they move, their color, and their shape. Do they resemble anything? Share what you see. You can liken clouds to your thoughts (see page 27)—sometimes fluffy, sometimes turbulent, always changing and moving.

TAKE FIVE MINDFUL WALKING

Walking is a wonderful way to integrate mindfulness into your everyday life and has been practiced as a meditative technique for thousands of years. Paying attention to the body as you walk will help you to enjoy simply being alive. This meditation is best done outdoors and even a five-minute mindful walking meditation is beneficial, although it is best to build up to 20 minutes when possible.

Before you start walking, bring your attention to your body. Take a few deep breaths and focus your awareness on your breathing. Then allow your breathing to settle back into its natural rhythm.

Now draw your awareness to how your body is feeling.

As you start to walk at a relaxed pace, continue to be aware of the sensations within your body. For once, you are not noticing what is going on around you, but you are drawing your attention inwards. How relaxed are your muscles? Notice the way you place your foot heel-first and then toe. How does the weight change from foot to foot as you move? Are your arms swinging? Do your shoulders drop as you relax? What's happening with your breath now? If you feel tension anywhere in the body, let it go.

It is easy to become distracted by your surroundings. If your mind wanders, gently bring your attention back to your body and the simple act of taking one step after another. Gently placing your full attention on the alternating steps of your left and right feet naturally brings about a meditative state.

An indoor variation of this exercise—or one for the garden (I like to do it barefoot)—is to go through this process but slow it down even further and take ten extremely slow steps in one direction before turning round and retracing your steps at the same pace, all the while drawing your awareness to the sensations within your body.

Encouraging Greater Freedoms

It is a natural instinct to try to keep your precious child safe. Yet, wrapping them in cotton wool and obsessively micromanaging your children's lives is actually sabotaging their development. Research consistently shows that children need free play, they need space to make mistakes and work out their own solutions if they are to grow into happy, resilient, and confident adults—and this includes giving them space to fail.

FREE
PLAY

MAKE
MISTAKES

WORK OUT
SOLUTIONS

Getting Outside

Inject some fun into your own family time with the kids in the great outdoors. Jumping in puddles, bike rides, rambles, flying kites in the park: being outdoors helps to ground us and to be present and mindful of the wonder of nature.

Like most mindful parenting, overcoming the temptation to be a "helicopter" parent involves inner work on yourself. It is commonly your own fears rather than rational concern for your child that trigger an overprotective, reactive response. Anxiously shrieking "Be careful!" as your child climbs a tree will make you feel better but simply serves to undermine your child's confidence: far better to occasionally ask if she is having fun, and surreptitiously spot her below in case of a slip.

Similarly, showing your children how you handle the unexpected, whether it's in normal life or in an outdoor environment, helps them to work out their own reactions when their hoped-for outcomes do not manifest. How do you react when your train is canceled or you get lost when map-reading on a hike? Are you flummoxed and angry or do you show that you can adapt?

You don't have to allow your children to roam the streets without supervision to give them greater freedoms. Perhaps you can find ways for your kids and their friends to play outdoors or in nature with the appropriate age-related supervision, but without interference and direction. Let them do it their own way.

(11) DIFFICULT TIMES

Few people envisage just how drastically their lives will change when they become parents. Nothing can prepare you for how much love you will feel for your children, how much being a parent will change you, how vulnerable and out of your depth you may feel, and just how stressful this new responsibility can be.

Of course, the joy that you experience from having children in your life—their innocence, joie de vivre, quirkiness, and unconditional love—makes it all worthwhile. But if ever there was a time when the stress of parenting and the magnitude of your role are felt most keenly, it is when major difficulties and tragedies come to call.

This is when the principles of mindful parenting can be of the utmost help in handling the chaos and emotion that often arise in such situations, but also when it is hardest to implement their calming benefits.

Handling Change

Whether it's starting a new school or moving to a new locality, change can be unsettling for your child—even if the change is bringing improvement. You may think a bigger house is wonderful, but your child may dread the move, despite having a larger bedroom. This is entirely natural.

"UNCERTAINTY IS THE ONLY CERTAINTY THERE IS . . ."

—JOHN ALLEN PAULOS, PROFESSOR OF MATHEMATICS, TEMPLE UNIVERSITY, PHILADELPHIA

Your children's anxiety may reveal itself in their behavior, so be mindful of subtle (and not so subtle) changes in mood when change is imminent. Although children often adapt quickly to new circumstances, in traumatic situations such as parental divorce, reactions may surface later. You can support your child through change by listening to their fears without dismissing them. Your child needs to know that however dramatic the change you will be there for them to turn to, so establishing secure connections when they are young is vital.

TAKE FIVE HANDLING CHANGE MINDFULLY

Suggest to your children that when they find themselves worrying about forthcoming change, they can notice that it is happening and gently say to themselves, "Come back." Then, they can take a couple of calming breaths and refocus on what they are doing right now in the present.

Another good way to be present and to stop needless worry about impending change is by practicing the Three Senses exercise:

Tell your child to take three slow breaths and then to ask himself:

- What are three things I can hear?
  (Ticking clock, bird song, my breath.)

- What are three things I can feel?
  (Carpet under my feet, chair under
  my legs, breeze on my face.)

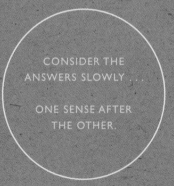

CONSIDER THE
ANSWERS SLOWLY . . .

ONE SENSE AFTER
THE OTHER.

- What are three things I can see?
  (Cat in the garden, passers-by
  outside, picture on the wall.)

This exercise will bring your child back to the present
and alleviate the worrying.

Handling Loss and Grief

Most adults are familiar with the experience of loss of a loved one and the feelings of grief that ensue. It is a natural process that helps us to make sense of the parting from a deceased loved one. Children also respond to loss with feelings of grief but it can be in response to various situations that may not affect you in the same way: a lost favorite toy, the death of a pet, when a long-term babysitter leaves, or when time with a parent changes after a divorce, for example.

"WE CAN HANDLE ANYTHING WHEN WE EXCHANGE OUR WORRIES AND FEARS FOR ALERTNESS AND SPONTANEITY, WHEN WE FOCUS SOLELY ON WHAT IS IN FRONT OF US."

—KAREN MAEZEN MILLER,

ZEN TEACHER AND

AUTHOR

Reflective Statements

You can help kids to process loss by reflecting their experiences, using reflective statements. When the babysitter has just retired, you might say, "Mary has always looked after you. You probably feel sad that she has had to finish. Do you wish you still went to her house every day?" When a favorite toy is lost, you may say, "We bought you Floppy when your baby brother arrived. You probably miss Floppy. Are your other toys not as important to you?" Or after a divorce, "It must be hard to get used to Mummy and Daddy living in different houses. Does it upset you when you can't decide where you want to sleep?"

Even if you consider an experience insignificant, if it is important to your child, by reflecting back their story, checking in on them, and leaving the door open for further communication at any time, you can help them to make sense of their distressing experience.

You can help your child to process grief and to make sense of the experience so that it does not have a continued disruptive influence on your child's life by telling her the story of the events and experience from her own perspective, making sure you focus on her feelings and not how you feel or the way you'd like her to feel.

DEALING WITH SADNESS

It is normal to feel sad occasionally, yet it is a hard emotion for children to handle and even harder for parents to witness. Naturally you want to help your children past their uncomfortable feelings, but you don't want to give them the message that it is a bad emotion or that they have to suppress or deny it. Give them a safe opportunity to notice, accept, and express their sadness to you or to themselves. In this way, the sadness often dissolves naturally.

When you suspect or know your child is feeling sad try the following:

- Find a quiet time to ask her if she is feeling churned up inside and if she'd like to talk or to cry, or does she want to be alone?

- Reassure her that it's OK to cry and that these feelings will not last indefinitely.

- Talk about how you feel when you are sad and what you do to make yourself feel better—go for a walk, listen to happy music, bake your favorite cake, do the gratitude exercise to remind yourself of happier times.

- You can talk about a movie or book with a storyline that involves a sad character or event. Discuss how the characters might have felt.

- Ask your child to draw what sadness feels like in her body. What color is it? How does a sad face look? This opens up a discussion on how you can tell when someone else is sad and the fact that it is natural for everyone.

Sometimes, children find it difficult to talk about feeling sad, and you may have to coax them into sharing. Yet, if you are able to listen and accept your child's sadness when he shares his feelings without the need to solve anything, it will help your child to realize that all feelings are valid. Sharing feelings and getting them acknowledged by you can take away the loneliness of sadness.

Difficult Times

Bullying

Every year, one out of every four schoolchildren reports being bullied and with the rise in cyber bullying and sexting, this figure is set to rise.

If your child is on the receiving end of unkindness or bullying, he may feel isolated and vulnerable. By confiding in you, your child has taken the first important step. Firstly, reassure your child that it is not his fault, and then contact the school and possibly organizations set up specifically to support people who have problems with bullying.

There is also a lot you can do to help your child to deal with the bullies and their own self-image. Empathy practice has been shown to play a vital role in preventing bullying and it can help your child to be more resilient in the face of unkindness. Research shows that children who develop empathy are more likely to intervene if they witness bullying and to stick up for vulnerable children.

"MINDFULNESS PRACTICES HELP THE BULLY, VICTIM, AND ANY WITNESSES INVOLVED DEVELOP A DEEPER AWARENESS OF THEMSELVES, RESILIENCE, COMPASSION, AND A GREATER ABILITY TO REGULATE THEIR EMOTIONAL RESPONSES."

—JANICE HOULIHAN, THE UNIVERSITY OF MASSACHUSETTS, BOSTON

SELF-ESTEEM PRACTICES

Victims of bullying need to learn to love or like themselves again after the loss of self-esteem which may result from being bullied. Help your child to find little ways to bolster self-respect and self-love.

Encourage your child to take time to sit quietly and observe her thoughts with detachment.

Offer her some positive affirmations that she can say to herself every day, such as, "I am my own person, I have boundaries, I am strong and centered." Or, "I have the right to be happy and free from fear." Let your child come up with her own affirmations that resonate with her particular circumstances.

Encourage your child to cultivate relationships with other trusted adults who care about her, as having a rich network of adult and peer relationships that involve healthy communication helps children to develop empathy and resilience.

12 KEEPING ON TRACK

No parent is perfect and there are times when we simply do not have enough inner strength or external support to be as connected and mindful with our children as we would like. This is the reality of parenting.

If you find that there are episodes in your family life where you slip back into your old, less grounded ways of parenting, that does not make you a bad parent. Mindful parenting is not easy and when you are stressed out, you can fall off the mindful parenting wagon.

The good news is that you can get back on at any time. Sometimes you have to work on yourself—getting grounded and present again—before you can reconnect with your children. Whatever challenges you face, whether they are acute crises or long-term difficulties, mindfulness practice—paying attention to your needs as well as your child's, being present without judgment—is the goal that you can set your sights on.

Compassionate Living

Modern family life is so time-pressed that many parents can scarcely fit in time for all the activities, commitments, and social events. Yet, with a little extra effort, you'll be surprised at how you can find a way to get involved with your children in projects that make a meaningful contribution to others.

Talk with your children about what causes resonate most with them. Tell them about what most moves you. It might be homelessness or disability, animal protection or the environment, the arts or politics . . . Whatever it is, why not look for a way to dedicate some of your precious time to volunteer as a family and to give something back.

SELF-COMPASSION PRACTICE

Most parents are their own harshest critics, especially when they slip back into old practices. This practice helps you to change how you judge yourself.

- In a quiet moment, think about a close friend who is struggling in some way and consider how you would respond to your friend in this situation. Then write down what you might do or say, and how you might talk to your friend.

- Now think about an occasion when you were struggling. How did you respond to yourself in that situation? Write down what you did and said to yourself.

- Can you notice a difference? If so, ask yourself why. Why do you think you treat yourself and others so differently? Write down how you think things might change if you responded to yourself in the same manner you respond to a friend who is suffering.

- Next time your inner critic starts up, think about treating yourself like a good friend!

Feeling Weighed Down

When it all gets too much and you're in danger of abandoning your mindfulness approach, try these techniques:

• If you are feeling disconnected from your child, focus on the essentials. Make sure they're fed and hugged and buy yourself a little time for some self-work.

• Find support from someone you trust who will listen compassionately and not try to fix things. Even asking for a hug from a loved one can make it feel better.

- Practice self-compassion and self-kindness—give yourself a break; does it really matter if you haven't done the ironing? Take some time for contemplative thought or meditation instead.

- When you do your gratitude exercise at bedtime, make sure you include some things that you appreciate about yourself as well.

- If you blow it with your child, don't panic. If, in the moment, you catch yourself losing it, stop, breathe, and start again. If you realize after the event that you mishandled a situation, remind yourself that we are all flawed and that you will do it differently next time. You might want to apologize to your child and tell them what you meant to say …

- Never give up on your child, even if she is behaving abysmally. Keep the vision of your child at her best in your heart and keep offering your love. Remember, it's the behavior that you don't like and that your child is not a bad person.

Every day is a fresh day, and an opportunity to connect mindfully with your child. Be present and pay attention to your interactions and, on balance, you will find that you make more love-based decisions rather than reacting out of fear.

Staying Connected

The key to staying connected and to getting back on the wagon when you slip is self-awareness.

By knowing what you think and feel, and how your thoughts and feelings influence your actions and choices, you are better able to understand your reactions to your child's behavior and to tune in to your child.

When you become mindful of why certain things press your buttons, perhaps by establishing a regular meditation practice or by developing the habit of checking in with your body and thoughts, chances are you'll think before you react. Self-awareness helps you to deal with the negative imprints and old patterns that you have amassed from your own life experiences, to shift your perspective, and to avoid passing on a negative legacy to your own children.

Once you recognize that reacting angrily to your child is simply a primordial brain response to a perceived stress, you can use mindful self-awareness to regain control and to bring you back to clear thinking.

TAKE FIVE · SELF-AWARENESS PRACTICE

On a daily basis, get into the habit of taking
five minutes to pay attention to yourself with
curiosity and compassion. Slow down your
breathing, stop everything else you are doing,
and check in with yourself.

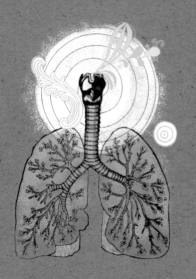

Tune in to your body with a quick body scan.
Are you storing tension in your shoulders?
Do you have tightness in your calves or lower
back? You store your emotions in your
body—so noticing any tension or tightness
can help you to get in touch with what you
might be experiencing emotionally. Then
remember to relax your shoulders, shake out
your legs, and open up your chest.

By increasing your self-awareness through daily practice,
you get a better sense of what triggers you, what are your
stressors, what is a legacy from your past. Armed with this
information, you can regain your equilibrium and feel
empowered to be the kind of parent you want to be.

Remembering the Good

When you are going through a tough phase in your family relations, it can feel as though you are constantly criticizing or nagging your child, which makes you and them feel bad. You may still need to make that complaint, but you can neutralize the negative impact by looking for the positives in your child and acknowledging those too. Throughout the day, if you tell your child that you appreciate random acts and gestures, it shifts you away from fixating on all that's wrong and toward celebrating what is amazing.

No Labels

During difficult episodes in family life, take a moment to watch your child when he is sleeping. Put the things that he is good at and those that drive you to distraction out of your mind; stop thinking of your child as James or Becky, with all the associated labels. Briefly step out of your role as parent and simply see the child as another spirit on this Earth sharing a journey alongside you. Enjoy this special moment.

This exercise is a great way to strip away names, labels, and egos, and to reconnect with who we are and the pure souls of our children.

It's also worth remembering that sometimes your child's behavior is only a problem because your thinking mind mistakes your mental reactions for reality. You think your child being wilful, throwing a tantrum, or being a picky eater is the problem, but it is only a problem if you believe your child should be well-behaved at all times. If you can step out of wanting and just notice the behavior, and accept it without judgment, you and your child are then both in the here-and-now and your relationship can flourish.

"NO ONE HAS YET REALIZED THE WEALTH OF SYMPATHY, THE KINDNESS, AND GENEROSITY HIDDEN IN THE SOUL OF A CHILD. THE EFFORT OF EVERY TRUE EDUCATION SHOULD BE TO UNLOCK THAT TREASURE."

—EMMA GOLDMAN

Conclusion: Loving Kindness

The most important component in any parent–child relationship is love. It is the cornerstone of your relationship. Even when things are tough and you feel like you're getting it wrong much of the time, if you always try to interact with your child from a place of love and with kindness, you cannot go far wrong.

I hope that you will find some or all of the ideas and exercises in this book useful and thought-provoking. Becoming more mindful as parents—gaining a better insight into who we are and who our children are—can be a joyful and illuminating journey, and one which I hope you will enjoy.

TAKE FIVE | LOVING KINDNESS PRACTICE

Let's end our journey together with another loving kindness (*metta*) practice. This is a meditation you can practice on your own or you can share with your child, getting them to join in and expand the circle of those you would like to send well wishes to.

It is a good idea to start by sending loving kindness to someone who loves you—your child, a partner, or a parent—before bringing the focus to yourself. Then you successively widen the circle of goodwill to those closest to you. If you are doing the practice with your child, take it in turns to name those whom you would like to benefit.

Continue widening the circle to those whom you feel neutral toward, then those with whom you have difficulties, and eventually end up with all living beings. Use phrases that are meaningful to you—and keep them simple.

Say out loud and carry on . . .

"MAY MY CHILDREN BE HAPPY. MAY THEY STAY HEALTHY. MAY THEY REMAIN SAFE. MAY THEY FEEL LOVED."

"MAY I FEEL HAPPY. MAY I STAY HEALTHY. MAY I REMAIN SAFE. MAY I FEEL LOVED."

Index

About the Author

Claire Gillman is an experienced journalist, editor, and writer based north of Manchester, England. She is the editor of *Kindred Spirit* magazine; she has also written on parenting, alternative health, and spirituality for many women's magazines, *The Times,* and other national newspapers. In the past, she was the editor of a number of consumer and specialist women's magazine titles including *Health & Fitness* magazine. Claire has written over 25 books, including *Best of Boys: Helping Your Sons through their Teenage Years, You and Your Ageing Parents: How to Balance Your Needs and Theirs,* and *The Healing Therapies Bible.* She is an editor and mentor for Writers' Workshop and runs writing workshops and retreats.